Name_____

Solve each problem in the list below. Use × and = to find the same problems hidden in the puzzle. Circle each hidden problem. Some of the problems share a number.

examples:

(3	× 2	=	6)	4	8	1	0	3	8	24	10	6	8	5
× 7	0	5	3	6	7	1	9	3	8	9	6	9	54
= 21	2	8	6	7	3	5	3	4	5	20	7	1	0
9	6	7	0	0	2	9	8	3	9	0	4	2	6
9	6	2	26	8	34	45	5	1	27	4	9	42	6
1	4	4	18	0	30	8	0	8	4	22	8	16	36
6	5	48	8	5	56	4	5	6	20	64	72	10	4
3	16	8	4	32	10	6	9	48	13	4	24	8	2
3	10	34	12	5	1	5	0	15	29	0	2	2	4
9	3	19	5	31	6	2	35	1	6	23	18	9	8
28	4	1	4	10	0	21	9	27	8	2	16	4	18
16	1	26	7	3	4	12	5	6	45	13	8	6	32
2	0	0	8	47	9	12	3	30	9	18	25	14	6
5	4	37	16	9	36	19	17	11	6	2	17	36	2
10	20	0	7	11	5	22	0	37	54	8	24	0	12

Problem List

2 × 0 = ____   3 × 2 = ____   9 × 6 = ____

3 × 4 = ____   3 × 7 = ____   3 × 3 = ____

5 × 1 = ____   3 × 8 = ____   4 × 1 = ____

8 × 6 = ____   5 × 9 = ____   0 × 8 = ____

9 × 8 = ____   7 × 0 = ____   4 × 5 = ____

2 × 2 = ____   6 × 9 = ____   6 × 2 = ____

1 × 4 = ____   2 × 4 = ____   8 × 4 = ____

2 × 5 = ____   8 × 2 = ____   6 × 6 = ____

4 × 9 = ____

1

Name_____

Solve each story problem.

a. Mrs. Sweettooth made 5 cookies for each of the 9 children in her family. How many cookies did Mrs. Sweettooth make in all?

_____ = _____

b. John Sweettooth and his dog Bowser like to eat cake. They each ate 2 pieces of cake. How many pieces of cake did they eat in all?

_____ = _____

c. Mrs. Sweettooth made 6 cakes. She put 6 cups of flour in each cake. How many cups of flour did Mrs. Sweettooth use altogether?

_____ = _____

d. John gave 4 cupcakes to each of his 9 friends. How many cupcakes did John give to his friends altogether?

_____ = _____

e. Jimmy put 2 eggs in each of the 8 cakes that he made. How many eggs did Jimmy use altogether?

_____ = _____

f. Katie put 1 teaspoon of vanilla in each of the 5 bowls of frosting she made. How many teaspoons of vanilla did Katie use in all?

_____ = _____

g. There were 9 girls in Sandy's Girl Scout group. Each girl made 6 cookies. How many cookies did the girls make altogether?

_____ = _____

Answer Key: a. 45   b. 4   c. 36   d. 36   e. 16   f. 5   g. 54

Name _____

Solve each problem in the list. Use × and = to find the same
problems hidden in the puzzle. Circle each hidden problem.

examples:

(9 × 1 = 9)

(8 × 3 = 24)

6×7= ___	5×3= ___
5×1= ___	6×4= ___
3×5= ___	4×4= ___
2×0= ___	2×4= ___
6×0= ___	8×6= ___
1×2= ___	1×6= ___
9×1= ___	7×8= ___
8×3= ___	3×8= ___
4×1= ___	9×4= ___
7×0= ___	4×8= ___
3×7= ___	8×8= ___
7×3= ___	5×5= ___
9×5= ___	

Puzzle:

```
48   1   5   3  15   7   5   2  21   2   0   0
27  12   4   2   7   2   8   0   9   5   7   2   4  22   4
 4   8   4   6   4  24   7  25   8   9   5   8  45   8
 6   8   3   2   5  37  19  43   1   7   5  27   8  14
 8  64   2   4   1   4   8   4   3   1   6   6   7   3
20  37   1  24   5  21  18   5  23   4  81   4   2   6
 6  48  11  46   9   7   0   0  10   3   1  36  18   0
 7  11   4  24   1  36   8  21   9  26   7   3  11   8   0
 2   7   9   3   5  15   1   6   3   6  21   6   4   8   1
 0   5  28   4   9   2  16   1   7   6   2   7   4   8   6
 4   8  32   6  13  49  36   9   2   5   9   4  16   4   7
 1  11   3   7   3  21   9  10   4  12   4   2  25   5   4
 5   4  19  44   6   8  20   7   8   5  36   3   6   7  42
 1   3   7   8  56   4   9   1   3   0  22   5   5   3   0
 5  15   4   0   5   9   1   2   2  40  12   3   8  24  10
```

3

Name_____

Solve each story problem.

a. Joey uses 8 towels each time he washes his dad's car. He has washed his dad's car 3 times this week. How many towels did he use in all?

_____ = _____

b. Bob washed 9 cars today. Tony washed 4 times as many cars as Bob washed today. How many cars did Tony wash?

_____ = _____

c. Jim uses 6 buckets of water to wash his dad's car. He washed his dad's car 4 times this week. How many buckets of water did Jim use altogether?

_____ = _____

d. Pam, Sue and Debbie each washed 7 cars today. How many cars did they wash in all?

_____ = _____

e. Patty used 6 jars of wax last week to wax cars. This week she used 7 times as many jars of wax as she did last week. How many jars of wax did she use this week?

_____ = _____

f. Jay's baseball team washed cars all day yesterday to raise money for new uniforms. They washed 8 cars during each of the 8 hours they worked. How many cars did they wash in all?

_____ = _____

g. Mike spent 7 minutes cleaning the front window on his dad's car. Julie cleaned the back window. She spent 8 times as many minutes as Mike cleaning the window. How many minutes did it take Julie to clean the back window?

_____ = _____

Answer Key: a. 24   b. 36   c. 24   d. 21   e. 42   f. 64   g. 56

Name________________________________

Solve each problem in the list below. Use × and = to find the same problems hidden in the puzzle. Circle each hidden problem.

Problem List

9 × 9 = ____	2 × 9 = ____
8 × 2 = ____	8 × 0 = ____
6 × 1 = ____	0 × 7 = ____
9 × 7 = ____	7 × 5 = ____
5 × 6 = ____	6 × 8 = ____
4 × 8 = ____	5 × 5 = ____
9 × 2 = ____	7 × 7 = ____
6 × 7 = ____	4 × 3 = ____
5 × 0 = ____	3 × 2 = ____
8 × 9 = ____	1 × 9 = ____
3 × 6 = ____	5 × 9 = ____
2 × 4 = ____	6 × 3 = ____
7 × 2 = ____	

examples:

9 ×	5	5 ×	5 =	25	3	7	7	49
9 =	6	5	24	11	6	16	31	8
81	7	0	4	3	7	40	2	0
5	3	0	11	18	42	60	12	0
8	81	4	3	12	84	3	2	6
2	55	10	9	2	18	3	56	1
16	11	10	6	3	18	13	4	4
7	5	2	16	7	1	0	8	11
17	6	26	7	5	35	9	32	3
5	30	21	0	8	4	6	56	2
2	1	16	9	7	63	31	5	9
6	9	7	2	14	4	0	2	18
8	1	3	7	36	8	9	72	0
48	4	6	6	41	17	5	28	0
61	0	18	5	13	5	9	45	6
0	7	0	7	1	4	18	71	1
46	2	51	3	6	2	4	8	6
15	1	9	9	3	7	9	1	18

Name_____

Solve each story problem.

a. Smitty made 3 snowmen. His sister Sandy made twice as many snowmen as Smitty. How many snowmen did Sandy make?

_____ = _____

b. It took the boys 7 days to build a snowman. They worked 2 hours each day. How many hours did it take the boys to build their snowman?

_____ = _____

c. Mrs. Coldspell made 5 cups of hot chocolate for the children. She put 6 marshmallows in each cup. How many marshmallows did she use in all?

_____ = _____

d. Jo, Jim, Don, Bob, Sue and Jill each rolled 3 snowballs so that they could each make a snowman. How many snowballs did they roll in all?

_____ = _____

e. Julie's snowman is 1 foot tall. Jim's snowman is 9 times taller than Julie's snowman. How many feet tall is Jim's snowman?

_____ = _____

f. There are 4 children in the Frost family. Each child made 3 snowmen. How many snowmen did the Frost children make in all?

_____ = _____

g. Susan made 5 snowmen with the help of her friends. They need 9 pieces of coal for each snowman's face. How many pieces of coal will they need in all?

_____ = _____

Answer Key: a. 6   b. 14   c. 30   d. 18   e. 9   f. 12   g. 45

Name _____

Solve each problem in the list. Use × and = to find the same problems hidden in the puzzle. Circle each hidden problem.

examples:

(0 × 2 = 0)

(6 × 9 = 54)

Puzzle grid:

6	8	2	1	56	2	6	12	1	64	0	1
3	6	3	6	13	5	36	8	3	3	9	
1	3	0	7	42	1	3	23	6	51	1	
14	41	21	14	11	74	3	2	4	8	5	
4	5	4	20	6	7	9	63	6	5	1	
2	13	6	1	6	0	33	12	1	31	5	
8	21	1	7	0	5	29	6	5	30	71	
43	2	1	6	6	7	7	49	7	11	3	
4	4	16	61	0	53	8	9	6	54	2	
9	0	8	0	3	10	1	7	0	6		

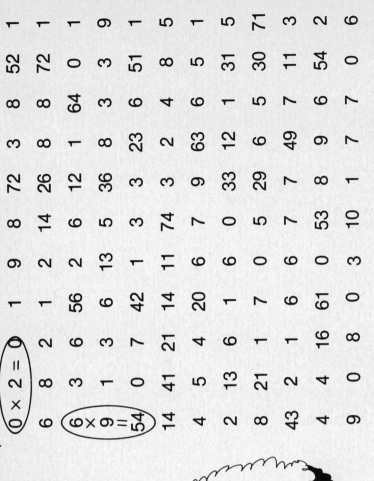

Problem List

0×6=	8×8=	1×3=	2×4=
4×4=	9×8=	6×1=	5×4=
7×7=	0×2=	2×1=	9×6=
8×1=	2×6=	3×3=	6×9=
0×8=	1×1=	4×2=	3×2=
1×7=	3×7=	5×1=	6×5=
			7×9=

Name _____

Solve each story problem.

a. Andy can pick 4 bushels of apples in an hour. How many bushels can Andy pick in 4 hours?

_____

b. Andy's cat picked 5 apples. Andy picked 4 times as many apples as his cat. How many apples did Andy pick?

_____

c. When Andy's cat threw the apples out of the tree, 6 apples landed in the bushel basket. Five times as many apples landed on the ground. How many apples landed on the ground?

_____ = _____

d. Andy uses 8 apples to make a batch of applesauce. When Andy's mother makes applesauce, she uses 8 times as many apples as Andy. How many apples does Andy's mother use to make applesauce?

_____ = _____

e. Andy's cat filled her basket with 7 apples. Andy filled his basket with 9 times as many apples as his cat. How many apples are in Andy's basket?

_____ = _____

f. Andy and his cat can pick 7 apples in a minute. How many apples can they pick in 7 minutes?

_____ = _____

g. Andy filled 3 bushels with apples on Monday. Tuesday, he filled 3 times as many bushels as he did on Monday. How many bushels did Andy fill on Tuesday?

_____ = _____

Answer Key: a. 16   b. 20   c. 30   d. 64   e. 63   f. 49   g. 9

Name _____

Solve each problem in the list. Use × and = to find the same problems hidden in the puzzle. Circle each hidden problem.

Problem List

4 × 7 = ___	1 × 5 = ___	6 × 5 = ___
9 × 5 = ___	0 × 4 = ___	5 × 3 = ___
8 × 7 = ___	6 × 2 = ___	5 × 8 = ___
7 × 4 = ___	9 × 6 = ___	2 × 3 = ___
6 × 9 = ___	9 × 1 = ___	9 × 3 = ___
4 × 5 = ___	4 × 2 = ___	
7 × 8 = ___	1 × 7 = ___	
5 × 2 = ___	8 × 1 = ___	
3 × 4 = ___	0 × 9 = ___	
7 × 1 = ___	7 × 6 = ___	

examples:

(3 × 4 = 12)

(6 × 5 = 30)

```
4   30   2   11   5    2   10   3    5
5    9   11   4    5   20    5   8    3
7    1    2   3    6    6   12  66   15
71   9    0   4   12    9    3  27    0
0    2   12   7    3    7    8  56    4
10   9    6  54   12   21    5    3
8    7   56   1    9    5   45   6    6
5    3   72   2    9    5    2  15   60   9
11  20    7   4   28   18    0   4    0  54
8    0    9   0   41    4    2  11    9   7
7    6   42  42    5   17    7   1    7   8
5    1   66  40   10   10    0   7    9   5
3    0    6   2   12   21    1   5    5   8
1    6    4   8   11    8    1   9   25  40
7    9    4   7   28    1   35   4   10  50
7    0    1  31    3    8    6   4    2   8
```

Name_____

Solve each story problem.

a. Hungry Hank can build a fire with 5 twigs of wood. Slim Sam builds a fire using 8 times as many twigs as Hank. How many twigs of wood does Sam use to build a fire?

_____ = _____

b. Hungry Hank can start a fire in 9 minutes. His friend takes 3 times as long as Hank to start a fire. How many minutes does it take Hank's friend to start a fire?

_____ = _____

c. Slim Sam can only eat 1 hot dog. Hungry Hank can eat seven times as many hot dogs as Sam. How many hot dogs can Hank eat?

_____ = _____

d. The first night the boys camped, they cooked 5 hot dogs. The next night, they cooked 3 times as many hot dogs as the night before. How many hot dogs did the boys cook the second night?

_____ = _____

e. It takes 6 minutes to cook a small hot dog. A large hot dog takes 9 times as long to cook as a small hot dog. How many minutes does it take to cook a large hot dog?

_____ = _____

f. A small hot dog can feed 1 person. A large hot dog can feed 5 times as many people as a small hot dog. How many people can a large hot dog feed?

_____ = _____

© Carson-Dellosa Publ.

Answer Key: a. 40 b. 27 c. 7 d. 15 e. 54 f. 5

Name_____

Solve each problem in the list below. Use × and = to find the same problems hidden in the puzzle. Circle each hidden problem.

examples:

(6 × 5 = 30)	7	36	3	4	12	8	6	4	24	3
10	(6	18	7	71	14	2	4	5	20	8	14	6
1	× 2	62	8	18	0	20	1	18	9	17	3	18
5	= 12)	4	56	7	4	6	24	10	52	15	8	1
5	9	5	7	33	9	66	3	30	7	5	35	4
25	36	70	3	8	4	32	8	7	52	9	0	4
3	5	6	36	50	6	12	63	3	7	0	22	16
2	71	9	22	6	5	2	10	21	10	0	70	2
1	60	8	11	27	18	16	5	20	1	5	24	11
2	4	72	4	5	7	35	5	0	0	7	42	2
9	1	9	32	7	8	1	9	6	54	6	40	3
11	8	62	3	30	6	6	4	21	3	1	39	6
4	3	12	1	0	48	7	62	8	2	16	1	74

Problem List

4 × 4 = ____   9 × 1 = ____   5 × 5 = ____

3 × 6 = ____   8 × 6 = ____   8 × 2 = ____

2 × 1 = ____   7 × 3 = ____   2 × 3 = ____

4 × 3 = ____   5 × 0 = ____   9 × 8 = ____

9 × 6 = ____   6 × 2 = ____   5 × 7 = ____

4 × 5 = ____   4 × 6 = ____   9 × 0 = ____

6 × 5 = ____   3 × 4 = ____   8 × 4 = ____

7 × 8 = ____   6 × 4 = ____   7 × 5 = ____

                                             5 × 2 = ____

Name_____

Solve each story problem.

a. Bob Bubbles can stay under water 9 minutes using his old air tank. With his new air tank he can stay under water 6 times longer than he could with his old air tank. How many minutes can Bob stay under water with his new air tank?

_____ = _____

b. Bob walked 3 fish today. Tomorrow, he will walk 4 times as many fish as he walked today. How many fish will Bob walk tomorrow?

_____ = _____

c. Bob and his fish friends have fun blowing bubbles. The fish can blow 8 times as many bubbles as Bob can in a minute. Bob can blow 6 bubbles in a minute. How many bubbles can Bob's fish friends blow in a minute?

_____ = _____

d. On Monday, while walking his pet fish, Bob spotted 5 different varieties of fish. Tuesday, he spotted 5 times as many varieties of fish as he did on Monday. How many varieties of fish did Bob spot on Tuesday?

_____ = _____

e. Bob walks his fish in water that is 4 feet deep. Once each week, he walks his fish in water that is 6 times deeper than the water he usually walks in. How deep is the water that Bob walks his fish in once a week?

_____ = _____

f. Bob saw 9 yellow fish. He saw 8 times as many orange fish as he saw yellow fish. How many orange fish did Bob see?

_____ = _____

g. Bob goes for 6 walks under water every week. How many walks will Bob go on in 2 weeks?

_____ = _____

12   **Answer Key:**   a. 54   b. 12   c. 48   d. 25   e. 24   f. 72   g. 12

Name _____

Solve each problem in the list. Use × and = to
find the same problems hidden in the puzzle.
Circle each hidden problem.

Problem List

4 × 0 = ___	0 × 0 = ___
3 × 1 = ___	2 × 3 = ___
5 × 9 = ___	4 × 6 = ___
8 × 9 = ___	3 × 9 = ___
1 × 5 = ___	7 × 0 = ___
2 × 8 = ___	0 × 1 = ___
4 × 8 = ___	4 × 9 = ___
8 × 5 = ___	5 × 2 = ___
1 × 9 = ___	6 × 0 = ___
6 × 6 = ___	9 × 1 = ___
7 × 1 = ___	7 × 3 = ___
2 × 9 = ___	5 × 4 = ___

examples: ⟨0 × 0 = 0⟩

Puzzle:

```
 2  ⟨6 × 6 = 36⟩  7  62   7   0   7
 5   16  11  40  21   8   3   9   1
 3   13   1   9   9  16  21   8   7
11    5   9  45  51   2   0  35   7   3
60    1  45  12  13  10   0   1   0   6
 9   15   4   7   2   3   6  66  65   0
 1   21   6   3   3   7  55  14   5   0
 9   11  24   8   1  66   3   9  27  21
26    9  55  14   3  17   8  32  11   6
 7    0   0   3  20   4   0   0  66   8
10   31   7   9   7  12  44  17  20   5
 4    5   4   8   9  72   3   0   2  40
 8    4   6  61   0  17   1   5   5  11
 5   20  18   5   2   5  11  26   7   4
 4   10  33  15   8  25   5   2  10   8
 9   36  13   3  16   7   9  22  14  32
 4    9  36   0  30   2   9  18  50   8
```

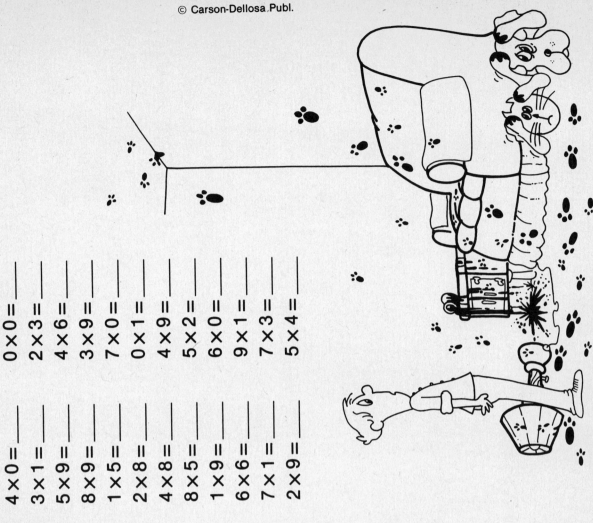

13

Name_____

Solve each story problem.

a. Bowser spilled 2 bottles of ink. Inky spilled 3 times as many bottles of ink as Bowser. How many bottles of ink did Inky spill?

_____ = _____

b. Inky left 6 pawprints on the carpeting. Bowser left 6 times as many pawprints as Inky. How many pawprints did Bowser leave?

_____ = _____

c. Patient Peter looked in 5 stores for ink remover. His mother looked in twice as many stores as Peter. In how many stores did Peter's mother look for ink remover?

_____ = _____

d. After leaving ink tracks on the carpet, Inky hid for 8 minutes. Bowser hid for 5 times as many minutes as Inky. For how many minutes did Bowser hide?

_____ = _____

e. Peter's mother scrubbed the carpet for 2 hours. Peter scrubbed the carpet 8 times as many hours as his mother. How many hours did it take Peter to scrub the carpet?

_____ = _____

f. The ink wore off the bottom of Inky's paws after 3 days. The ink stayed on Bowser's paws 9 times as many days as it did on Inky's paws. How many days did the ink stay on Bowser's paws?

_____ = _____

g. Inky made 4 paw prints. Bowser made 8 times as many paw prints as Inky. How many paw prints did Bowser make?

_____ = _____

Answer Key: a. 6   b. 36   c. 10   d. 40   e. 16   f. 27   g. 32

Solve each problem in the list. Use × and = to find the same problems hidden in the puzzle. Circle each hidden problem.

Problem List

0×6 = ___	1×8 = ___	1×1 = ___
8×7 = ___	7×9 = ___	6×0 = ___
8×8 = ___	9×4 = ___	7×7 = ___
6×6 = ___	9×5 = ___	4×7 = ___
3×2 = ___	3×5 = ___	2×5 = ___
6×7 = ___	2×8 = ___	7×1 = ___
8×0 = ___	4×9 = ___	3×1 = ___
9×3 = ___	8×5 = ___	7×4 = ___
4×8 = ___		

examples: (6×7=42) and (7×4=28) are circled in the puzzle.

Number-search puzzle grid:

7	9	63	9	14	0	4	17	6	0	0	11	8
61	2	1	6	1	3	14	6	8	13	5	8	
33	17	7	5	2	51	1	13	2	8	16	64	
7	×	4	=	28	34	6	76	36	3	70	6	17	7
5	8	15	2	20	16	4	8	32	12	9	0	
7	3	5	4	7	28	55	12	19	7	20	4	11
7	11	16	2	4	9	3	6	56	9	36	3	
49	6	7	1	7	1	31	5	9	4	5	12	19
71	8	25	5	12	1	13	15	3	10	2	5	10
5	0	6	6	36	1	11	41	3	1	3	5	9
14	0	12	36	4	40	17	8	0	12	6	10	45	5
1	9	8	5	40	1	9	6	21	1	3	6	45
21	16	6	32	24	8	7	0	18	7	2	8	38
10	9	3	27	31	8	0	9	4	35	4	9	36

(6×7=42) is also circled in the puzzle as an example.

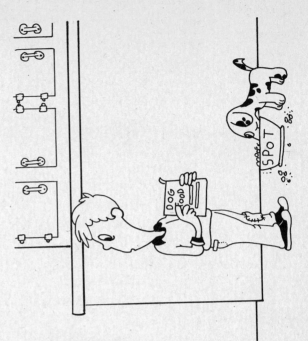

Name _____

Solve each story problem.

a. Yesterday, Ralph's dogs ate 3 bowls of dog food. Today, they will eat 5 times as many bowls of dog food as they ate yesterday. How many bowls of dog food will Ralph's dogs eat today?

_____ = _____

b. Ralph bought 4 bags of dog food for his puppies. His mom bought 9 times as many bags of dog food as Ralph. How many bags of dog food did Ralph's mom buy?

_____ = _____

c. Ralph's dogs were so happy to see him that they each gave Ralph 7 kisses. Ralph has 4 dogs. How many kisses did Ralph get altogether?

_____ = _____

d. Ralph's dogs like to eat bones. He has 2 dogs. Each dog ate 5 bones today. How many bones did they eat altogether?

_____ = _____

e. Three of Ralph's puppies needed shots. Each puppy needed 2 shots. How many shots did Ralph's puppies need altogether?

_____ = _____

f. Ralph's puppies get fed 4 times each day. How many times will Ralph's puppies get fed over 8 days?

_____ = _____

g. Ralph has saved 6 dollars. He needs 6 times as many dollars as he already has to buy each of his puppies a collar. How many dollars does Ralph need altogether to buy each of his puppies a collar?

_____ = _____

© Carson-Dellosa Publ.

Answer Key: a. 15   b. 36   c. 28   d. 10   e. 6   f. 32   g. 36

Name _____

Solve each problem in the list. Use × and = to find the same problems hidden in the puzzle. Circle each hidden problem.

examples: (9 × 8 = 72)   (8 × 3 = 24)

```
7   3   8   2   5  10   2   0   3   0
6   4  24  72   4   5   1   5   6   3
9  74   9   1  21   4   1   4   6   2  61   8
11  2  11   3   5  15  12  10  62   1   9   6
52  7   6  81   2  19   2   8   3  16  48
5  14   8   4   9  36  12   2   5   3  12   1
9   2   4  12  71   3  71   4   6  24  51
4  64  32   1   7   0   0  16   2  15  36  11
36  5   8  10   9  31   8  10   0   2   0   7
1  81   0   6   0   5   8   2  52   9   0   0
2   6  12   9   8  42  64  71  13  81   2   0
32  5   7  35   4  13   3   3  81   1  41   7   8
7  11  22   7   9  63  13   2   0   0   7   0
```

Problem List

9 × 8 = ____	8 × 6 = ____
7 × 9 = ____	4 × 1 = ____
0 × 3 = ____	2 × 5 = ____
8 × 4 = ____	0 × 8 = ____
1 × 3 = ____	4 × 6 = ____
2 × 0 = ____	5 × 7 = ____
3 × 5 = ____	0 × 2 = ____
8 × 3 = ____	6 × 4 = ____
2 × 2 = ____	9 × 0 = ____
8 × 8 = ____	5 × 1 = ____
4 × 9 = ____	2 × 6 = ____
0 × 6 = ____	9 × 4 = ____
7 × 0 = ____	

Name_____

Solve each story problem.

a. Roger Bait caught 7 fish. His cat friends caught 9 times as many fish as Roger. How many fish did the cats catch?

_____ = _____

b. Fluffy the cat fished for 2 hours last week. Roger fished 5 times longer than Fluffy. How many hours did Roger fish?

_____ = _____

c. Roger uses 4 worms every hour he fishes. How many worms does Roger use in 6 hours?

_____ = _____

d. Roger bought 4 earthworms to use as bait. He bought 9 times as many night crawlers as he bought earthworms. How many night crawlers did Roger buy?

_____ = _____

e. Roger only had 8 bites on his fishing line all day. The cats had 8 times as many bites as Roger. How many bites did the cats have on their fishing lines?

_____ = _____

f. Fluffy caught a fish that was 2 inches long. Roger caught a fish 6 times as long as Fluffy's fish. How many inches long was Roger's fish?

_____ = _____

g. The cats went fishing 8 times last summer. Roger went 3 times more often than the cats. How many times did Roger go fishing?

_____ = _____

Answer Key: a. 63 b. 10 c. 24 d. 36 e. 64 f. 12 g. 24

Name _____

Solve each problem in the list. Use × and = to find the same problems hidden in the puzzle. Circle each hidden problem.

examples:

(8 × 4 = 32)

(0 × 9 = 0)

Problem List

4 × 3 = ____	9 × 9 = ____
0 × 9 = ____	6 × 3 = ____
4 × 7 = ____	2 × 7 = ____
5 × 6 = ____	8 × 6 = ____
8 × 2 = ____	9 × 3 = ____
1 × 4 = ____	3 × 4 = ____
7 × 5 = ____	7 × 8 = ____
6 × 7 = ____	5 × 3 = ____
3 × 8 = ____	1 × 2 = ____
0 × 5 = ____	9 × 5 = ____
8 × 4 = ____	7 × 3 = ____
6 × 6 = ____	5 × 5 = ____
0 × 3 = ____	

Puzzle Grid

18	14	11	6	22	6	7	42
22	9	7	6	3	18	6	7	14	1	17
8	5	6	30	62	8	36	8	2	10	0
9	5	45	3	21	2	7	56	9	61	3
2	16	21	5	5	25	51	10	2	6	0
5	3	2	7	14	81	13	2	9	3	27
41	4	3	12	4	3	7	1	2	9	3	72	6
1	9	52	8	5	4	1	31	11	7	3	21
4	4	81	11	1	12	15	7	19	0	1	32
7	3	3	8	24	12	42	5	14	5	15	5
28	1	13	9	81	71	35	20	0	32	3
1	4	4	3	16	12	8	6	48	5	10	15

19

Name _____

Solve each story problem.

a. Cara Catchall caught 8 times as many fish as her brother Carl. Carl caught 7 fish. How many fish did Cara catch?

_____ = _____

b. Carl fished for 2 hours. Cara fished 7 times as many hours as Carl. How many hours did Cara fish?

_____ = _____

c. Cara got 7 nibbles on her line. Carl got 5 times as many nibbles on his line as Cara. How many nibbles did Carl get on his line?

_____ = _____

d. Carl's largest fish weighed 4 pounds. Cara's largest fish weighed 3 times as much as Carl's fish. How many pounds did Cara's fish weigh?

_____ = _____

e. Cara went fishing 9 times during summer vacation. Carl went fishing 9 times more often than Cara. How many times did Carl go fishing?

_____ = _____

f. Cara's fish weighed 3 pounds. Carl's tire weighed 4 times as many pounds as Cara's fish. How many pounds did Carl's tire weigh?

_____ = _____

g. Cara saw a school of 9 fish. Carl saw a school of fish that had 5 times as many fish as the school Cara saw. How many fish were in the school of fish Carl saw?

_____ = _____

Answer Key: a. 56   b. 14   c. 35   d. 12   e. 81   f. 12   g. 45

Name_____

Solve each problem in the list. Use × and = to
find the same problems hidden in the puzzle.
Circle each hidden problem.

9 × 3 = ___	3 × 2 = ___
8 × 0 = ___	2 × 7 = ___
7 × 6 = ___	2 × 9 = ___
6 × 2 = ___	9 × 8 = ___
5 × 4 = ___	8 × 7 = ___
4 × 3 = ___	4 × 5 = ___
3 × 4 = ___	2 × 6 = ___
9 × 7 = ___	7 × 9 = ___
7 × 1 = ___	8 × 2 = ___
4 × 6 = ___	6 × 8 = ___
8 × 4 = ___	7 × 4 = ___
6 × 5 = ___	5 × 8 = ___
5 × 6 = ___	

examples:

(9 × 3 = 27)   1   3   9   7   63

51   2   7   83   6   4   6   2

(9
×
8
=
72)   9   10   8   7   56   7   61

7   3   71   3   14   6   7

13   2   7   14   4   42   1

2   8   2   16   11   3   32   7

5   9   6   2   6   4   11   81

6   6   2   43   8   3   8   3

30   14   12   21   48   12   6   11

1   41   5   16   8   4   32   10   23   7   13   2   9   18

5   4   20   8   4   73   12   9   11   6   1   17   53   3

63   1   32   8   33   4   5   20   78   5   66   7   4   28

2   6   12   5   8   40   5   31   2   30   6   7   9   63

9   1   3   6   13   5   36   8   8   3   2   6   4   8

54   0   1   42   0   3   3   3   4   12   17   6   1   0

14   41   21   14   11   74   3   2   4   6   24   9   10   0

© Carson-Dellosa Publ.

Name _____

Solve each story problem.

a. Henry Hound can wash 4 boys in an hour. How many boys can Henry wash in 3 hours?

_____ = _____

b. Henry put 6 capfuls of bubble bath in his bath water. Clarence put 5 times as many capfuls of bubble bath in his bath water as Henry. How many capfuls of bubble bath did Clarence use?

_____ = _____

c. Clarence Clean soaked in the tub for 4 minutes. His brother soaked 5 times as long as Clarence. How many minutes did Clarence's brother soak in the tub?

_____ = _____

d. Henry needs 9 gallons of hot water for each tub. How many gallons of hot water does Henry need for 7 tubs?

_____ = _____

e. It takes Henry Hound 2 hours to get ready for each bath. How many hours will Henry need to get ready for 6 baths?

_____ = _____

f. Henry Hound washes Clarence Clean 4 times a week. How many times will Henry wash Clarence in 6 weeks?

_____ = _____

g. Henry Hound takes a bath 7 times a year. Clarence Clean takes a bath 9 times as often as Henry. How many baths does Clarence take in one year? (Henry Hound could be cleaner!)

_____ = _____

Answer Key: a. 12   b. 30   c. 20   d. 63   e. 12   f. 24   g. 63

Name_____

Solve each problem in the list. Use × and = to find the same problems hidden in the puzzle. Circle each hidden problem.

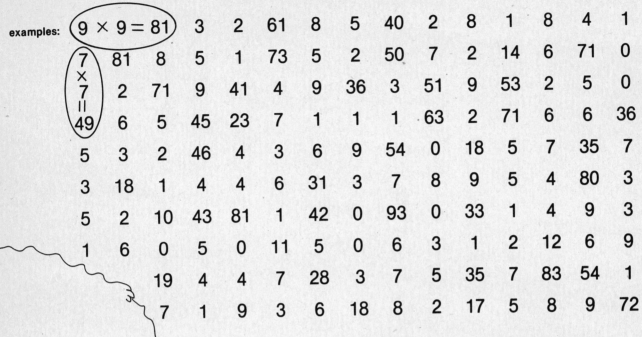

examples:

9 × 9 = 81	3	2	61	8	5	40	2	8	1	8	4	1
7 × 7 = 49	81	8	5	1	73	5	2	50	7	2	14	6	71	0
	2	71	9	41	4	9	36	3	51	9	53	2	5	0
	6	5	45	23	7	1	1	1	63	2	71	6	6	36
5	3	2	46	4	3	6	9	54	0	18	5	7	35	7
3	18	1	4	4	6	31	3	7	8	9	5	4	80	3
5	2	10	43	81	1	42	0	93	0	33	1	4	9	3
1	6	0	5	0	11	5	0	6	3	1	2	12	6	9
	19	4	4	7	28	3	7	5	35	7	83	54	1
	7	1	9	3	6	18	8	2	17	5	8	9	72

Problem List

9 × 9 = ___	8 × 1 = ___	1 × 1 = ___
5 × 7 = ___	6 × 3 = ___	8 × 9 = ___
4 × 9 = ___	4 × 7 = ___	5 × 9 = ___
1 × 0 = ___	3 × 6 = ___	0 × 8 = ___
9 × 6 = ___	7 × 2 = ___	3 × 3 = ___
0 × 5 = ___	5 × 2 = ___	8 × 5 = ___
7 × 5 = ___	1 × 4 = ___	7 × 7 = ___
		9 × 2 = ___
		3 × 0 = ___
		6 × 6 = ___
		6 × 9 = ___

Name _____

Solve each story problem.

a. Joey raked 6 piles of leaves. His dad raked 3 times as many piles as Joey. How many piles did Joey's dad rake?

_____ = _____

b. Dad whistled 1 tune each time he raked a pile of leaves. He raked 7 piles of leaves. How many tunes did Dad whistle?

_____ = _____

c. The boys ran through 9 piles of leaves on Monday. On Tuesday, the boys ran through 2 times as many piles of leaves as they did on Monday. How many piles of leaves did the boys run through on Tuesday?

_____ = _____

d. Jeff tossed 8 leaves into the air. Joey tossed 9 times as many leaves into the air as Jeff. How many leaves did Joey toss into the air?

_____ = _____

e. Joey raked yards for 7 days. Jeff raked yards 5 times as many days as Joey. How many days did Jeff rake yards?

_____ = _____

f. Jeff filled 6 trash bags with leaves. Dad filled 6 times as many trash bags as Jeff. How many trash bags did Dad fill?

_____ = _____

g. There are 3 trees in Joey's front yard. There are 3 times as many trees in Joey's back yard as there are in his front yard. How many trees are in Joey's back yard?

_____ = _____

Answer Key: a. 18 b. 7 c. 18 d. 72 e. 35 f. 36 g. 9

Name _____

Solve each problem in the list below. Use × and = to find the same problems hidden in the puzzle. Circle each hidden problem.

examples:

(1 × 8 = 8)
(4 × 1 = 4)

1×8=8	5	1	81	1	9	4	36	7
35	9	5	7	35	0	76	22	2	5	16
4×1=4	0	43	1	11	78	8	3	6	18	0
13	9	6	11	1	3	5	16	6	4
2	1	12	8	21	53	7	0	4	28
5	14	8	6	2	12	3	2	32	9	36
10	21	7	15	7	5	17	6	4	24	14
0	42	3	7	6	42	20	9	15	11	7
5	8	40	4	8	7	56	83	9	8	4
25	17	20	6	61	5	4	1	0	51	5
8	9	63	8	16	0	31	7	0	4	20
0	10	5	3	19	1	9	13	3	40	2
0	7	5	24	6	2	9	7	63	5	7
41	9	2	18	3	10	0	26	3	6	2
12	54	6	8	48	73	18	0	7	0	14

Problem List

0 × 7 = _____	3 × 5 = _____
7 × 2 = _____	2 × 2 = _____
1 × 8 = _____	1 × 6 = _____
3 × 6 = _____	0 × 4 = _____
5 × 7 = _____	9 × 2 = _____
6 × 2 = _____	8 × 7 = _____
7 × 4 = _____	7 × 6 = _____
8 × 0 = _____	6 × 8 = _____
2 × 5 = _____	9 × 4 = _____
4 × 1 = _____	9 × 7 = _____
9 × 0 = _____	8 × 3 = _____
6 × 4 = _____	5 × 8 = _____
4 × 5 = _____	

THE DOCTOR is iN

Name _____

Solve each story problem.

a. Dick's ambulance service received 7 calls last week. This week it has received 2 times as many calls as it did last week. How many calls did Dick's ambulance service receive this week?

_____ = _____

b. Dick used 8 bandages on Spot's front leg. He used 3 times as many bandages on Spot's back leg as he did on his front leg. How many bandages did Dick use on Spot's back leg?

_____ = _____

c. Dick can pull his ambulance wagon 2 miles each minute. How many miles can Dick pull his wagon in 5 minutes?

_____ = _____

d. Dick treats 6 dogs every day. How many dogs does Dick treat in 2 days?

_____ = _____

e. Spot had 1 bandage on his left leg. His right leg had 6 times as many bandages as his left leg. How many bandages were on Spot's left leg?

_____ = _____

f. Dick can make it to the hospital in 5 minutes from Spot's house. It takes Dick 8 times as many minutes to get to the hospital from Rover's house as it does from Spot's house. How many minutes does it take Dick to get from Rover's house to the hospital?

_____ = _____

g. Dick uses 2 boxes of bandages each month. How many bandages will Dick use in 2 months?

_____ = _____

Answer Key: a. 14 b. 24 c. 10 d. 12 e. 6 f. 40 g. 4

Solve each problem in the list. Use × and = to find the same problems hidden in the puzzle. Circle each hidden problem.

examples:

(8 × 1 = 8)

(6 × 3 = 18)

20	9	1	51	8	48	6	5	30		
3	7	21	2	6	62	6	21	12		
1	24	4	2	8	7	7	81	7		
14	5	3	15	54	72	5	1	32	18	42	8	1
4	1	52	15	11	42	0	18	2	6	0	0	7
6	1	4	4	16	51	0	3	12	7	39	8	17
24	5	15	27	1	2	6	12	16	2	22	9	36
61	5	0	4	21	8	3	24	2	14	60	7	41
2	9	18	42	3	57	10	6	5	7	35	2	1
33	5	0	30	6	45	7	5	35	0	3	21	3
7	7	49	31	18	6	0	7	0	7	9	63	3

Problem List

2 × 9 = _____   4 × 4 = _____   5 × 7 = _____
3 × 7 = _____   5 × 0 = _____   7 × 2 = _____
1 × 3 = _____   8 × 3 = _____   8 × 6 = _____
5 × 3 = _____   7 × 5 = _____
0 × 7 = _____   6 × 5 = _____   8 × 1 = _____
6 × 0 = _____   7 × 1 = _____   6 × 3 = _____
4 × 6 = _____   1 × 5 = _____   3 × 6 = _____
2 × 6 = _____   7 × 9 = _____
7 × 7 = _____

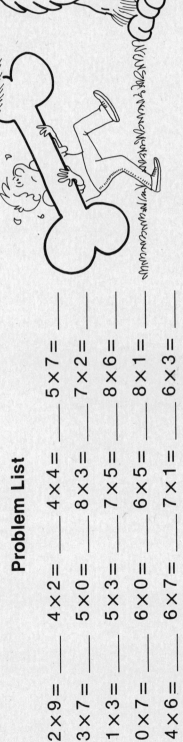

Name _____

Solve each story problem.

a. Fido stole 5 bones from the museum today. Yesterday, he stole 7 times as many bones as he did today. How many bones did Fido steal from the museum yesterday?

_____ = _____

b. Eight of Dino Dinosaur's bones are loose. The museum keeper has already repaired 3 times as many bones on Dino. How many bones has the museum keeper repaired on Dino?

_____ = _____

c. Donna Dinosaur has 4 bones in her skeleton. Dino Dinosaur has 6 times as many bones in his skeleton as Donna. How many bones does Dino have in his skeleton?

_____ = _____

d. Fido has gathered 3 bones from the museum. In order to share his bones with his friends, he needs 6 times as many bones as he already has. How many bones does Fido need in order to share with his friends?

_____ = _____

e. Fido buried 7 dinosaur bones today. Next week he will bury 7 times as many bones as he did today. How many bones will Fido bury next week?

_____ = _____

f. Dino Dinosaur has 7 long, pointed teeth. Donna Dinosaur has 9 times as many long, pointed teeth as Dino. How many long, pointed teeth does Donna have?

_____ = _____

g. Fido buried 6 bones behind the garage. He buried 5 times as many bones in the front yard as he buried behind the garage. How many bones did Fido bury in the front yard?

_____ = _____

Answer Key: a. 35 b. 24 c. 24 d. 18 e. 49 f. 63 g. 30

28

Name _____

Solve each problem in the list. Use × and = to find the same problems hidden in the puzzle. Circle each hidden problem.

examples:

(5 × 5 = 25)   (0 × 4 = 0)

```
3    2    4   (5 × 5 = 25)   8   16    3    9   27    2    5   20
(0 × 4 = 0)    1    7    2    8   28    6   49    2    7   14   18
28    3   35    9    1    8   64    3    7    4   28   28    7    8
12    7    4    9    3    4   18    4    5    4   20    1    7    5
25    8   45    0    2    3    4    8    4    1    5    2   24   40
 8   56   32    3    0    8   32    0    6    4   24    3    8
 0    6    0    1   45    4   16    6   45    4    0   32    0
 3    5   15    6    5    4    3    7    6    1    6   16    8    0
 6   20    1    6    3    7   49    3    1    9    2   18   20
 6    6   36    7   15    5    2    3    6    9    5   45    0    3
```

Problem List

0 × 4 = ___	0 × 6 = ___
1 × 9 = ___	6 × 4 = ___
1 × 6 = ___	7 × 4 = ___
3 × 5 = ___	2 × 3 = ___
4 × 4 = ___	8 × 5 = ___
4 × 8 = ___	5 × 5 = ___
5 × 3 = ___	7 × 7 = ___
2 × 7 = ___	3 × 0 = ___
6 × 1 = ___	6 × 6 = ___
5 × 4 = ___	3 × 9 = ___
9 × 2 = ___	8 × 8 = ___
8 × 0 = ___	9 × 5 = ___
7 × 8 = ___	

Name _____

Solve each story problem.

a. Bobby blew 4 bubbles for his younger brother before he ate dinner. After dinner, Bobby blew 4 times as many bubbles for his brother as he did before dinner. How many bubbles did Bobby blow after dinner?

_____ = _____

b. Bouncy Barbara owns 3 jars of bubble liquid. Bonnie Blower owns 5 times as many jars as Barbara. How many jars of bubble liquid does Bonnie own?

_____ = _____

c. Walter Windy can blow 7 bubbles a minute. How many bubbles can Walter blow in 7 minutes?

_____ = _____

d. Peter Pucker blew 5 giant bubbles on Tuesday. On Thursday, he blew 5 times as many giant bubbles as he did on Tuesday. How many giant bubbles did Peter blow on Thursday?

_____ = _____

e. Bobby's bubble floated 9 feet. John's bubble floated twice as far as Bobby's bubble. How many feet did John's bubble float?

_____ = _____

f. On Monday, Rover chased and broke 3 bubbles. On Tuesday, Rover chased and broke 9 times as many bubbles as he did on Monday. How many bubbles did Rover break on Tuesday?

_____ = _____

g. Lucy can blow 9 bubbles a minute. How many bubbles can Lucy blow in 5 minutes?

_____ = _____

Answer Key: a. 16   b. 15   c. 49   d. 25   e. 18   f. 27   g. 45

Name_____

Solve each problem in the list below. Use × and = to find the same problems hidden in the puzzle. Circle each hidden problem.

examples:

0×5=0	1	7	8	4	32	6	18	1	2	2
10	7	5	0	9	12	4	2	14	3	22	9	69
5	0	×2	2	12	5	8	40	32	3	11	4	2
56	13	=10	46	8	10	20	7	54	9	8	9	13
2	37	1	12	7	64	2	7	14	11	70	1	5
3	9	27	7	56	50	3	8	24	8	13	6	64
10	2	4	11	5	6	81	3	0	6	11	6	8
4	3	12	3	0	6	30	6	8	48	2	4	7
5	4	7	28	8	0	13	1	6	44	66	11	1
2	8	16	4	42	0	4	10	7	5	6	30	0
6	40	34	9	2	36	4	8	5	16	7	72	3
10	8	3	24	0	7	16	5	33	9	3	5	1
11	4	12	3	9	0	52	0	1	6	7	64	3
26	1	5	7	6	42	1	0	8	24	2	12	6
74	9	7	63	10	6	4	74	8	3	7	3	21

Problem List

0 × 5 = ___	1 × 2 = ___	6 × 0 = ___
5 × 2 = ___	3 × 3 = ___	3 × 1 = ___
1 × 6 = ___	9 × 7 = ___	4 × 4 = ___
3 × 9 = ___	2 × 7 = ___	5 × 6 = ___
6 × 8 = ___	5 × 0 = ___	3 × 8 = ___
8 × 7 = ___	4 × 3 = ___	7 × 6 = ___
7 × 3 = ___	5 × 8 = ___	4 × 7 = ___
2 × 8 = ___	8 × 3 = ___	8 × 4 = ___
		1 × 8 = ___

31

Name _____

Solve each story problem.

a. Scruffy brought Daisy dog bones for 3 days. He brought her 7 bones each day. How many dog bones did Scruffy bring Daisy in all?

_____ = _____

b. Joey's dog has 5 fleas. Martha's dog has 8 times as many fleas as Joey's dog. How many fleas are on Martha's dog?

_____ = _____

c. Cindy takes her dog Tiffy on a walk twice each day. Cindy and Tiffy have gone on walks for 7 days. How many times has Cindy walked Tiffy?

_____ = _____

d. Jo walked his dog 4 miles today. Tomorrow they will walk 7 times as many miles as they walked today. How many miles will they walk tomorrow?

_____ = _____

e. Snippy and Nicci always go on walks together. They walked 8 blocks today. Tomorrow, they'll walk 4 times as many blocks as they did today. How many blocks will they walk tomorrow?

_____ = _____

f. Sam barked for 9 minutes yesterday. Today he barked 7 times longer than he did yesterday. How many minutes did Sam bark today?

_____ = _____

g. Gail gave her dog 5 bones today. Dave gave his dog twice as many bones as Gail's dog received. How many bones did Dave's dog receive?

_____ = _____

Answer Key: a. 21   b. 40   c. 14   d. 28   e. 32   f. 63   g. 10